Am I Enough for You?

By Trina Olson

© Copyright 2022 – Trina Olson
All rights reserved. This book is protected by the copyright laws of the United States of America. This book may not be copied or reprinted for commercial gain or profit. The use of short quotations or occasional page copying for personal use is permitted and encouraged. Permission will be granted upon request.

Unleashed Publishing, Inc.
975 Wayne Avenue #351
Chambersburg, Pa 17201 We can be reached by calling (717) 860-1848 or through our Website:
unleashedpublishing.net

ISBN-13: 978-1-7356913-0-5
ISBN-10: 1-7356913-0-5

Second Revision

I would like to dedicate this book to Nic and Rachael Billman of Shores of Grace Ministries.

Nic and Rachael – your friendship is so precious to me. I am forever thankful for the example you set as laid down lovers of Christ.

Your worship melts hearts. It is like it fills the room, opening the atmosphere of Heaven and invading the hearts of everyone in the room. In those moments of incredible worship, the Presence of God encounters individuals, changing their lives forever.

As I stood in front of the altar that day in 2009, I experienced an encounter that changed my life forever. Seeing Jesus standing in front of me changed my perspective on how Jesus sees me, leaving a taste of Heaven that will linger continually drawing me deeper into His heart. Your worship ushered in the presence of God and opened the door for Jesus to invade my heart that day.

It has been a blessing to watch encounters with God guide and direct your lives, taking you to another country with young children and creating a ministry that changes lives all over the world. Extreme obedience and the power of an encounter with the one true living God, Jesus Christ, gives the strength to walk by faith.

Your lives emulate John 15:16 where Jesus says, "… you will bear fruit, lasting fruit." You are creating beautiful, on-fire children and spiritual children who are also fruitful. Keep running the race and finish well my friends.

Love you, Trina

Table of Contents

My Life Flashed Before My Eyes...................................7
Am I Enough for You?..11
The Vision... 15
    Points to Ponder 27
When You Walk in the Room 29
Walking out Obedience.. 39
My Journey Continues...41
Opportunities to Renew Your Mind..........................49
References..53

My Life Flashed Before My Eyes

And there before me was a door;
a door of life and not death;
a door of purpose and hope and not hopelessness;
a door of being embraced by a love I never
encountered before.

As I saw my car pulled off that embankment,
I saw the hand of God lift me up through the door
that was before me.

The beauty and elegance of life changed me into
who I never knew before!
As I looked, I saw the throne of God; the Father of
all Fathers, the majestic one who called me, Who
knew me before I was conceived,
My Father as He said, "Welcome Home my
beloved daughter."

A warmth covered me and drew me into
His presence creating a new temple inside of me.

A temple of God where He would now reside in
me with Jesus and we would be one.
One with Jesus who is one with the Father that we
would be in unity together in this one place that
gives me free access to the Heavenlies,
access to my Daddy.

A rainbow of promises encircled the throne of my heart where God sits, seeing Him tear down lies and restoring truth.

As I looked inward into my heart, I saw Heaven. As I went deeper, I saw God sitting on the throne of my heart and the twenty-four elders were enthroned around Him with a brilliance of white, calling forth my purity, calling forth my innocence to once again resound.

*Flashes of fire coming from the throne,
God burning away the dross in my heart,
to singe away the wounds and sores,
restoring it to how it was created,
my heart was conforming to the Father's heartbeat.*

*I saw a sea of glass before the throne.
Father God stepped down and asked me
to let Him teach me how to dance.*

*As I learned balance and grace
there was a weaving of wisdom growing in my strength, a strength from the Father, a touch of Heaven creating a tapestry of beauty and elegance in the mantle He placed on my shoulders.*

A tender kiss that lured me deeper and deeper into His heart.

His eyes were piercing fire going deep into my soul and calling forth life.

His hands gentle and strong, holding His baby girl once again.

"Am I Enough for You?"

These words still ring through my ears and I can still picture the day and the exact moment when Jesus asked me that question. I would like to paint you a picture of this moment and take you on a journey as God unfolds the revelation of this vision.

Is Jesus Enough for you? This is a question I want to instill inside of you as you read this book. My prayer is that the vision and encounter I had will enrapture you into the heart of the Father intensely as you encounter the arms of Jesus pulling you into Him. I pray that God will pour out revelation of His heart for you as you go on a journey with Him where you will encounter a deeper love of Jesus than you have ever encountered before. I pray God will take you into the depths of your own heart.

Picture this: You are young and on fire for God. You have a zeal that is uncontrollable. You are undone by the transformation God has done in your life over the past few years. You actually saw God turn your life around in a such a way that you will not be going back because now you have a divine plumbline in your life. You know what God brought you out of and you know for sure you are not going to go back to your old life. You have tasted the goodness of God and actually know that if it was not for that moment when God tangibly touched your life, you would not be living.

Picture this: A young person done with life yet God pulls you out of the pit of hell. You had given up and even quit wanting to live and it was only the hand of God that reached out to turn your life around.

Picture this: Someone so riddled with medical problems that you couldn't even function to make it one more day. In that moment when God turned your life around, He also removed depression and any hopelessness you were encountering.

Picture this: Someone who over the next year saw the hand of God take you on journeys into the wilderness to unveil His love for you; A love you had never encountered before. Someone who started to believe in something beyond your own comprehension. The scriptures began coming alive as you opened the Bible, seeing the stories play out as you read them. Everywhere you walked you saw or heard God talk to you through nature, through people, or even through the billboards of life as you walked into your new season of life.

Picture this: Someone who started to see the scriptures come alive more and more each day and who started to see God heal every one of your medical problems, one after another, over a nine-month period of time.

Picture this: Someone who learned the importance of obedience when they failed to speak to someone whom God put in front of them and then watched that person die a few months later through the hands of the enemy taking them out in a car accident.

Picture this: Someone who knew they were being called into ministry but had NO clue what that looked like! Someone whom God was unveiling their calling to while walking with them each step of the way.

This could be you! This could represent so many people who have had life changing encounters with God, where you suddenly know you are called into ministry, called into a new walk of life! What does it look like to step into ministry? To step into a life of being sold out for God? To have your eyes only on Jesus while stepping away from who you once were!

The Vision!

I was hungry and on fire for God. I was walking out a season of life that I had never even dreamed possible. I was at a conference in the spring of 2009. A moment in time which God used to change my life once again.

I was up front at the stage during the worship time giving my heart and my all to God. I was undone and so zealous for more. In that moment God, met me with an incredible encounter, changing my life and even the way I look at my destiny.

You see, I was a young woman who thought that as I walk out my call in life, I needed a husband. The world thinks you need a covering and I was in a church for over 18 years that didn't allow females to speak. I was looking for my husband, thinking it couldn't possibly be me that God really wanted to use. I dealt with unworthiness, insecurities, and rejection that stemmed from lies I was believing. I was believing that I was unloved and couldn't trust God or others to protect me. I was a mess but God wanted to use me anyway.

As I was worshiping and giving God my whole heart, an encounter unfolded before my eyes:

Jesus appeared like He was really standing in front of me. I was undone and melted into floor at the Altar. He leaned down and placed His hands gently on my face, lifting me to my feet. He looked-intently at me with such love, love I had never experienced before. I can still see His eyes piercing through my soul, deep into my spirit. As if Deep was calling out to Deep! (Ps 42:7)

The words I heard next forever changed my life. Jesus spoke to me saying, "Am I enough for you"? The question pierced my heart and pushed the darkness aside to shine light into the dark cavern of my heart. A bright light encapsulated my wounded heart. Tears streamed down my face. I said, "YES!" I felt like I was screaming from the inside out with such a gut wrenching cry. Again, as He continued to stare deep into my spirit pushing away more darkness in my heart, I heard those words again, "Am I enough for you?" I saw a deeper, more intense stirring in my heart as I saw the veil across my heart tear, unveiling the "YES" deep within me. Undone and broken, I felt the presence of His touch go deep into my heart pouring out once again the question, "Am I enough for you?" Those words rang throughout my entire being yet again as I was so undone I had nothing left and it was only a small, simple "yes" that came out of my broken and marred spirit. I felt His hands touch me in places hands can't touch. I felt Jesus penetrate every wall of pain, every offense, every bit of hurt I had ever encountered in that moment to reach the one He knew before I was even formed in my mother's womb. His hands picked up that little infant baby girl who once knew Him intimately and His hands held His baby girl once again.

My heart was undone and so full of a love I truly never encountered before. My "yes" was pure and untainted by the world or anything I had ever encountered in life. My "yes" was a yes that met His will for my life.

As I laid there in His arms feeling His intense presence, He looked intently into my eyes and asked me one more question. He said these words that reached deep into the depths of my spirit; "Trina, if I have no one else for you, am I enough for you?"

It was so surreal. I felt a pure reverence for God. The fear of God penetrated my spirit and I knew I had a choice: to go deeper into the deepest desires of my heart and come into perfect alignment with His spirit or merely continue onward as I was. I cried out a gut wrenching yell from the very pit of my spirit, yelling: "Yes, Yes, Yes if you have no one else for me, You are enough!!!!" My Yes met His Yes and I was never so full of His love than in that moment. My Yes became a part of who I was becoming. I was deeply affected by the presence of God, both emotionally and physically, and almost felt as if I was changed at a cellular level. My Yes was all He really ever wanted to hear from me to know that I put Him before every other part of my life.

As I exhaled all my "Yes", Jesus looked into my heart and said these amazing words as He began to speak life into my spirit. He said, "When I have you where I want you, I will bring your husband alongside of you." He continued, "You and he will catapult each other into your destinies. You have a destiny; he has a destiny; and together you both have a destiny. As a married couple, you will fulfill three destinies." As I lay there in His Presence, pondering the encounter, I was unable to move, unable to comprehend the magnitude of what I had just experienced. What did I just say Yes to and what will that look like? I was so in love with the one true living God, Jesus Christ. I just encountered His love in such a deep way that knew it would carry me through my life and give me wings to soar wherever He directs.

How does a person begin to comprehend what I had just encountered? How do you unpack something that significant in your life? What do you do next?

There were many questions that came to the surface as the days and weeks went on. As I walked out the days ahead, God kept showing me where people struggled time after time to empower others or to be empowered themselves. My heart broke to see women in leadership roles without any real authority. To see women mostly hidden away as intercessors or being used as a shield to protect their husband, the pastor. To see woman after woman being the dutiful wife, the submissive wife, holding down the homefront and being the prayer warrior when she was called to so much more. My heart broke time after time, seeing the women usually only in women's ministry or helping with the children, but rarely at the pulpit with their husband. Time after time I searched the heart of God for each one and would call out their greatness when God would open up the door for me to speak life to their dreams.

As a society we put a glass ceiling over women, limiting their upward movement, but it is breaking. Can you hear it? Shattering. Women have begun to break through and many are finding success. So many denominations don't feel women have a right to step up to the pulpit; I pray that feeling will change through scriptural revelation from the Holy Spirit. Our culture teaches us that if women are going to walk in ministry, they should have a strong Christian man with a call on his life so they can submit to him and be covered by him. We are quick to want young people to get married and excited to see "called" Christians connect, not considering they may not be called in the same direction. Many are failing to fully embrace what God has for them as the pull of a good Christian Marriage distracts them from pursuing their Destiny wholeheartedly.

What if we could do life differently? What if we would focus on directing young men and women to Christ first and foremost? He should be our covering and we need to keep our eyes on Jesus as the prize, not looking to the left or to the right. We need to focus on building our relationship with Jesus, God, and the Holy Spirit where we will hear God and know His voice. Then we will see where He is and go where He directs us and not be directed by a denominational doctrine or people. We need to be sold out for God, undone by His presence with Jesus overflowing in and through us. We need to disciple others to run their own race with Jesus, and not simply follow what other people are doing, but follow God's divine destiny for their own lives. As they follow the one true Shepherd, Jesus Christ, they will come into alignment with Heaven's plan, allowing God to bring the spouse He has for them into their lives; The spouse He has been preparing for them, the one who will understand the importance of walking out all three of their divine destinies.

What does that look like in the "real" world? What if God gave you a vision of what your future spouse looked like? Could you lay down searching for them, trusting God for the ultimate "meet and greet" and for the ultimate God ordained divine encounter with your soul mate?

After my encounter where Jesus asked me if He alone was enough for me, God opened my heart and He took away my desire for just any husband. I knew that He Himself was enough for me. He also helped me to understand a husband was being prepared for me at the same time He was also preparing me for my future husband.

Later that year, God took me on a mission trip to Brazil while attending Global Awakening's School of Supernatural Ministry. It was my first time flying into another country and I was excited. I was going, fully expecting God to show up and to show off mightily in and through my life. I wanted to see God use me. I wanted to come home a different person, transformed into the "new" Trina God was creating.

I got something I was not expecting.

During one of the impartation sessions during the ministry nights, I was "undone" and fell out in the Spirit and God showed me a critical piece of my future. I was taken into a vision where I saw a gorgeous, handsome guy. My eyes were taken to his piercing blue eyes as God introduced me to him. Jeramy was his name and I was speechless for the first time in a long time. I was undone by the love in his eyes, a love that pierced through my spirit, deep into my heart. As I looked at him, I saw his long jaw line complimenting his short, spikey blond hair. His beautifully tanned skin covered his bulging biceps. His arms were so huge but also so gentle as he embraced me. I met my soul mate, the love of my life. I felt like I had known Jeramy all my life and he was picked just for me; God had handpicked my husband to complete me.

Many years have gone by since that October day in 2009 while I lay on the floor of the large Brazilian church where God introduced me to my future husband. Many people heard about this Jeramy and many have asked time after time when is he coming, when will you meet your husband? God's timing is not our timing and the process is more important than seeing the promised vision fully manifest.

After this amazing encounter, two amazing men whom I highly regard spoke wisdom into me and their words gave me wings to soar through the process and to embrace the seasons as God unfolds my destiny. Both Max Myers and Randy Clark spoke at the second year graduation ceremony of The Global School of Supernatural Ministries in 2011. They both spoke in a similar context but each shared their own revelation from God. The understanding I received that day went something like this: You are in Plan A and you have vision of Plan D or E. You will need to go through the process of Plans B, C, and possibly D to see the manifestation of the vision you are seeing now. If you rush the process or even skip over some of the process, you could possibly miss the destination or misalign the vision.

So what if in going through your process you are to meet someone critical to the final outcome of the vision and by short cutting or short changing the process you miss meeting the critical person? Yes, God is bigger than our mistakes but it may take another person to come alongside of you to complete the vision in a different way and it could possible cause a delay. What if taking a short cut causes the vision to be aborted because you need to gain insight through the process and you miss out on the character growth necessary to sustain the dream? These are important questions to consider the next time you want to hurry the process along or even totally bypass the process because you think you know better than God.

We wonder all too many times why our visions and dreams never manifest. We think God is the reason and we are all too quick to point the finger, blaming God for not coming through on His promises for our lives. Take a moment to ponder on this and consider: What if God wouldn't allow the dream to manifest because you didn't allow for the growth of the spirit inside of you necessary to sustain the dream? What if God gave you that dream or vision and allowed it to fully manifest in your life without the needed moral fiber within you and the dream crushed you? God didn't let the Israelites enter into the Promised Land because they were not ready spiritually, so why would He let you enter into your promise unprepared? God loves us too much to allow extra opportunities for the enemy to take us out! The Israelites found freedom but not liberty; God delivered them from the slavery of the Egyptians but was unable to give them liberty. They couldn't get past their slave mentality and always thought of themselves as grasshoppers. They allowed fear to rule inside of them when they came against the only two men who saw themselves as conquerors who had truly been set free and could think as free men.

I would like to propose to you that if God had given the Israelites the liberty they wanted to run into the Promised Land carrying rebellion and fear and whatever else accompanied their slave mentality, the enemy would have "smelled them a mile away" and taken them out even if it was one at a time. Do you realize God loves us so much that He would rather we die in the wilderness, never tasting the goodness of the Promised land than have us see it and walk into the Promised land poorly prepared only to be taken out by the enemy by being thoroughly destroyed which would instill far greater fear in all of the people following you?

God recently told me that He is "building the character in me to sustain the dream He put in my heart". The dream which I have in my heart is huge and it needs God's hand to cover it.

I have read books and listen to many podcasts and videos of Aimee Semple McPherson, Maria Woodworth Etter, and Katherine Kuhlman. As I was watching them, I saw the ups and downs of women Revivalists pushing through their limitations in a culture where is was not acceptable for a women to be a Preacher. God raised up amazing Revivalists in these women and used them mightily, but it was not without significant struggles in their lives.

  As I heard their testimonies, I felt God speaking to my heart. He took me back to my encounter where Jesus was at the altar asking me, "Am I Enough for You? If I have no one else for you, Am I Enough for You?" A "Yes" came deep from within my spirit and I prayed a prayer that day; I prayed these words to God: "God, If the Jeramy you have for me will take my eyes off of you, I don't want him." I felt that the cost was too great for me to exchange my love for a human man for God's love and I didn't want to pay that cost. I want God,

Jesus, and the Holy Spirit to be number one in my heart and I want my eyes focused on Jesus and not a man. I had so much peace saying those words; Peace overwhelmed me from the top of my head to the bottom of my feet.

Once again I was undone by the touch from Jesus that day as I prayed that prayer. I was willing to give up my gift from God (the vision He showed me of my future husband) for God! I want Jesus above everything and everyone else. Paul said it is far better to be single (than married) in 1 Corinthians 7:7. Paul also states: "God gives the gift of single life to some." I am content with Jesus being my husband!

Points to Ponder:

Do you really trust God to provide your spouse for you?

If so, pray for an encounter to meet your future spouse and to give you the faith and ability to know they are a work in progress just as you are a work in progress.

What areas of your life is God working on or wants to work on in your life to allow character to be built to sustain the dream in you?

If you are married, how can you allow God to build a greater relationship with Him and your spouse so that your marriage will truly empower each other by launching each of you into your destinies?

If you are married, are both of you walking out each of your dreams or are you only walking out one dream? Even in a dream shared by both of you, are there areas that allow you each to fulfill the dreams God placed inside of each of you?

What does empowering your spouse look like in your life? Can you come alongside your spouse and empower them to be the greatest they can be in life? Is your spouse lifting you up and encouraging you to fulfill your greatest potential?

When You Walk in the Room!

"When you walk in the room, there is nothing like it. When you walk in the room, darkness starts to tremble." These words to a song came alive during a conference a few years ago when Jesus actually walked into the room and down through the crowd.

When You Walk into the Room!

Have you ever encountered Jesus walking into the room while you are standing, undone, worshipping Him with all your heart? Have you ever felt a burning in your heart like nothing else ever mattered?

Radical Launch International Ministries was birthed in such a moment! While standing and worshipping in a large crowd, everything stopped when He walked into the room. Angels were everywhere. As Jesus walked into the crowd, everything stopped and a burning desire consumed my heart. It was like a bowling ball hit the crowd as Jesus walked down through the middle of the crowd and people went down in the spirit as though the sea parted. There, before me, stood a 7-foot angel who touched my hand. Everything changed as I faded into an encounter. Nothing else mattered as I was consumed by the presence of God. Everything changed in my life!

As everything faded away, I melted into another realm where God took me to a barn in Franklin County, Pennsylvania. I literally found myself in the midst of the farm where the barn was located and I saw a man by the name of Harold that I would later come to know. I had passed the area where the barn was located many times, seeing the sign that pointed down the lane to it, but had never met Harold before. I was undone - one moment I was worshipping God in a Conference and the next moment, I found myself in another location in a vision.

As quickly as that vision came, it changed into another vision. In the second vision, I was seeing two barns in the area where I lived, full of young people and heard God saying: "Barn Raising Tour." I then saw barns all over Pennsylvania and then all across the Nation! The visions seemed to last forever but in reality, it was only a few minutes and then I was back in my body, lying on the floor of a Conference feeling the intense presence of God hovering over me.

I went home thinking about that amazing vision in which God actually gave me the name of the barn owner. What do you do with that kind of information? God didn't show me how to connect with the barn owner and God didn't give me any other information, but He kept this desire burning deep within me to pursue after something which I really had no understanding about what it all meant.

I visited two amazing friends of mine, Ben and Bev, about two weeks after having that incredible vision. While visiting them, I shared with them about the vision of the barns and the person I saw in the vision. Without skipping a beat, Ben picked up his cell phone and made a phone call. Without me even realizing it, he was contacted Harold. Within minutes, Ben was speaking to Harold about my vision. Only two weeks after having the vision, God was already bringing the necessary connections together. It is not about how we "make something happen", but rather it is ALL about what and where is God in the midst of things. I could not have even dreamed of what was about to transpire over the next few weeks. Ben and Harold had been friends over the years and God already knew this connection when God prompted me to hang out with Ben and Bev. God can make things happen and open doors no man can shut in the blink of an eye. As the two friends spoke, they scheduled a time for me to meet Harold the following week. Within three weeks of me having the vision, God was bringing the pieces of dreams together from several directions.

What does it look like to see a dream or vision walked out? How much will we know and how much do we need to simply trust and wait on God for His timing? These were some of the questions that kept running through my mind. The moment I had been waiting for was about to transpire after three weeks. What was I going to say? How was Harold going to respond? The possibility of this vision coming to life seemed so farfetched and crazy, but I knew it was real in my heart and I knew God was doing something. I could not even imagine what was about to transpire.

I was undone by God's goodness as I sat across from Harold, the barn owner who God had showed me in my vision. I was amazed how God gave a vision and without me really doing anything, it was unfolding before my eyes. I simply connected with friends God put on my heart and I just felt led to share with them my vision. When I was obedient with what I could have simply dismissed as my own thoughts, God brought forth the connections and was unfolding a plan to bring the vision alive. I had no clue to the fullness of what He was bringing forth. God had a plan where He was creating an environment that would be safe place for a community to come together to raise up a generation of youth! I don't feel the youth are a particular age but rather a generation of all ages and walks of life, that are young in the spirit but willing to lay down everything to run for God. God was establishing a place for people to practice the prophetic, teach, preach, worship, and pray where they would not be judged, but rather encouraged to keep seeking God's presence and to find a balance of Spirit and Truth in their lives. I felt God was showing a new concept of lifting up those He highlights to be Teachers and Preachers and He wanted to create an open environment where people could be free to unlock what was inside of them, revealing the person they were in the process of becoming.

We held our first "Worship in the Stables" gathering in May of that year and we began to see people being empowered. There were over 40 people worshiping in the barn that first night. Our group would select a speaker from within the group each month, unleashing the potential inside them and releasing the revelation God had been instilling inside of each one of those people. This group was different! As I looked around the inside of the barn on the first night of our gathering, I saw friends who believed in me as well as the vision God was giving me. I was undone by the amount of people who showed up to see what God was going to do that first night. As I walked to the back of the barn, I looked at the stage where the group breaking out in prophetic worship. God brought together many different worshipers along with their equipment. We had an amazing sound that ushered in the presence of God in a breathtaking way that night.

"Worship in the Stables" had a heart to lift up people from within the group to release the revelation God was pouring out in individuals through giving them a place to share their message. We all have a message to reveal Jesus to the world (John 17:20). In the Passion Translation it says: "And I ask not only for these disciples, but also for all those who will one day believe in me through their message." It is not about us preaching John 3:16 to the world by telling them that: "God so loved the world that He gave His only begotten son… ." That was John's message and while it is a message we can, it is not our message. Our message is revealed when we share what God did in and through our lives. That direct testimony will reveal the heart of the Father by bringing Jesus to life through our message. The heart of our particular group was to inspire others to know they hear the voice of God and that God is pouring out revelation through each of us as we connect with the heart of the Father. God wants us to get the Word of God in us so that we can reveal the heart of the Father and the love of Jesus through our messages, our lives, our words, and our actions.

As the gathering evolved on the very first night of "Worship in the Stables", it felt surreal as I stood in the back of the barn, watching it all play out before my eyes. I heard God say these words to me: "You think this just came together over the last few months, but I have been bringing this all together over the last four years of your life." I was in tears as I looked around and saw people who had come into my life over those four years, people whom we had built relationships with and who had impacted my life. I just wept, knowing the Love of the Father and how He sees the greater picture in our lives. This gathering continued for months as God poured out through the group. Eventually we changed the name to "Runway 4" and later the gathering was handed over to my mentor and best friend, Stephanie. She picked up the mantle and it to evolved into her vision as they pursued deeper worship by training people in prophetic prayer and worship. Watching this group evolve was incredible. Stephanie currently holds meetings once a month called "His Move" where they are pursing nonstop worship, seven days a week around the clock. Radical Launch International Ministries, Inc. is still holding similar meetings where we empower the Body of Christ to know they each have a voice to speak forth the messages God has instilled inside each of His sons and daughters.

Walking out Obedience

Months after these visions came to pass, the path of my life started to shift. So much had transpired over a short period of time in my life. How do you learn to walk out what God has in front of you? What does the path of your life look like for you? Have you experienced moments where you felt there was a huge shift in the direction you felt God was taking you? Sometimes the path God has for you looks different and it may cause others to question where you are going.

If you are walking in a direction with God and He suddenly changes that direction significantly, will you know it is God? Some would believe the vision from God should fully manifest before it changes directions or changes hands. Some people may even say I ran away from what God had started because I wasn't willing to see it through. No matter what others think, we need to know in our own hearts what God saying to us. When we stand before God someday, all those people around you will not be standing beside you. You alone will be held accountable before God, no one else: not your parents, not your siblings, not your spouse, not your kids, not your best friends, nor your mentors, and not even your Pastor. You and you alone are responsible for fulfilling your own life and completing what you are given by God. You will answer for what you do with what He has given you.

During this same season when God brought forth the "Worship in the Stables" Gathering from an encounter with Him during worship at a Conference, God was doing more in my life, more than I could ever imagine. My Mom who was my best friend passed away in October of 2011. It was an adjustment to say goodbye. As I was walking out of one season of my life, God was preparing me for the next season of my life where I would learn to depend solely on Papa God, where He would be my provider and I would learn to walk out obedience to Him and not to man. I was at another worship conference the next year and during impartation with the laying on a hands by a person for God to impart into you what you will need for the next season of your life. Several well-known speakers from the Conference prayed over me and as I felt hands laid on my shoulders, I felt the power of God touch my entire body and I fell down under the weightiness of the presence of the Lord. I went out in the Spirit as my knees went weak and I was no longer able to stand on my own. While laying on the floor, intense electricity flowed throughout my body and I felt an incredible fire well up inside of me. I didn't see much during this encounter, but I heard these words. I heard God say: "Get rid of everything". As I started to come out of the encounter, I remember wondering:

what part of everything is everything? I walked over to a few friends while still considering this encounter. As I approached my friend Sherri, she looked in my eyes and said, "I don't know what you just encountered but there is a white banner with black letters that reads 'CRUCIAL' over your head." She continued on to say, "You do not feel worthy for the call on your life." I collapsed in her arms and just wept. I knew the words I heard God speak in the encounter and I knew He was serious. Deep down inside, I also knew I didn't feel worthy of what God was calling me to do in my life. I had dealt with rejection, insecurity, and unworthiness for most of my life which had actually led me to suicide. When God had pulled my car off the embankment a few years earlier, He had said to me in an audible voice: "You can continue to be stupid, but I (God) have a plan for your life."

I had no idea what was about to transpire in my life. How do you get rid of everything? I had been given all the household stuff when my mom passed away minus a few personal items given to other family members. I was now renting a beautiful two bedroom, one car garage house filled with of lots of amazing stuff. Over the next few months, God started to take me on a journey to help me walk out obedience to the command: "Get rid of everything." I was headed to Brazil in March on a Mission Trip and as I was preparing for the trip, God told me that before I left on the trip I needed to give my notice for giving up my lease on the house. That was going to be hard, telling family and friends I was moving yet had not arranged where I would move. Telling family and friends I was getting rid of everything but had no specific plans for the future was crazy from the viewpoint of the world. Being a person who isn't confrontational, I waited until the very last minute to tell my brother who was my landlord that I was moving at the end of June.

My Journey Continues

God is amazing. He has given me the amazing support of friends who hold me accountable. Yes, God always provided help! As I was walking out that process, I experienced God's love. I have often been in tears as I saw God help me give to people who touch hearts all over the world. Wow! That is how awesome our God is, always bringing people to you that you need to meet. Oftentimes I did not know where I was going as I stepped this process out. God wanted to see if I would step out in faith, trusting Him above all else. It has not been easy. I heard many questions and had lots of doubt thrown my way. One friend said, "God would not take you out of one job without giving you another job." Another commented: "even Paul worked." It was actually iron sharpening iron, helping me to learn how to focus on what God was doing rather than on what people were saying. I had to wade through man's wisdom to get to God's Wisdom. It was one of the toughest times of my life.

What are people saying in your life that goes against what you feel God is saying?

As I continued to walk out my journey with God, I saw God show me many times how to destroy the path of the enemy. One of those times, God brought a friend into my life at the perfect timing to help me uncover a lie that I was believing. I shared with my friend that I had been struggling to understand an Encounter I had 2014 and that I felt it was key to revealing truth I needed to bring victory and freedom in an area of my life that was desperately needed. In the Encounter, I saw my body in a grave with the devil himself throwing dirt, shovel upon shovel, onto my body. With each load of dirt landing on my chest, I could feel my inability to breath and it became harder and harder to get a breath of air into my lungs. My breathing was becoming shallow and the pain felt real. The Encounter was as thought I was experiencing every moment of this in real life. While all of this was happening, my spirit was running around the top of the grave, trying to get my body out without getting caught in the grave itself. I was undone and had no answers, I had no more ability to help the one person I loved the most, myself. I hunkered down and cried out to God, saying, "God, I don't know what to do!" Immediately I saw Jesus carrying my body out of the grave - it was limp, laying across his arms. He looked at me and said, "It is not your own". I thought to myself: that is scriptural.

I then heard God speak these words: "if you don't stop adhering to what man says, that is what will happen to you." God then said, "you will lose your vision, your passion, your purpose, and then despair, discouragement, and depression will consume you and everything you have been healed of will come back with a vengeance." I was a weeping mess, laying on the floor at a youth Tent Revival Meeting in western Pennsylvania. I had gone out under the spirit of God during a time of prayer and God had taken me into an Encounter. As I was speaking to my friend much later on, I felt God take me back to those moments of that encounter and it was as if it had just happened.

My friend puts two chairs facing each other and has me sit in the one. He takes me through a series of questions and being led by the Spirit of God I find that root of my struggles. I saw myself as a 12-year-old little girl setting in that chair across from me afraid. Afraid of failure, afraid of letting others down. I went into an encounter and saw me being the 6th man on the basketball court being put in the stressful position of coming off the bench cold but expected to shine and not screw up. It is your moment to pick up where others may not be as strong in that moment because they need time to breath and regroup from being tired. Your time to understand every moment from this time is important and will be valued as you play. You could play your best or your worst and would it really matter?

You could score or you could foul, but the only thing that would really be remembered would be the moments you didn't perform up to the expectations of the team by being able to stay in the game until the first-string person could come back into the game refreshed, and full of a new burst of energy to go the extra mile. You were just a comma in the game, a pause, nothing more and nothing less. It didn't matter if you played your best, it was only a fleeting moment you had to be just a comma in the game. The Encounter I had then went into a moment where I was pinch-running for another player in softball. I could even feel the warm hot day and the pressure to perform. I could feel the sweat running down my back, not knowing if it was from the stress of being expected to perform or from the hot summer sun melting my back. I could smell the dust in the air and the french fries on the grill. Overwhelmed by the adrenaline piercing every atom of my body, the batter up at the plate unleashed a great hit. However, the ball was not hit far enough to let me run comfortably home, yet I knew that run would win the game. I knew when I rounded third base, I would hear the third base coach clear enough to know to go or to stop. As I rounded the base, my heart was racing so fast I could even hear it again now in my head, as though I could not hear anything else. I went for it as I didn't see the ball coming yet. I saw people jumping up and down and sensed an urgency to turn up the speed and to go low as I come to Home plate. Diving into the plate was my passion that was penetrating my entire being. Adrenaline was flowing deep into my soul as I came sliding headfirst into home plate with no concern for the consequences of the impact of my body hitting the ground. Swoosh into home, I just cleared the plate as the ball landed in the Catcher's glove. There was silence all around as we all waited for the response from the Referee. Seemed like forever! As the dust settled, I heard what seemed like far in the distance, "Safe! She is Safe!" The Referee's call piercing through my ears as I was covered with dirt. Excitement and an explosion of love picked me up for only a moment as my run scored the winning run. The Encounter ended as I saw myself in the very next game just sitting on the bench, watching everyone fill their regular spots while mine was yet again just warming the bench, just hoping to get one chance in the game to score a run.

As I have been led by the Spirit of God, I have come to understand that I often felt invisible; Invisible to the world and always struggling to be seen. I simply wanted someone to see me, someone to understand that I do exist. Nothing more, nothing less, just to be seen for who I was becoming. I have been on an ever-evolving journey, coming to know who I am in Christ and knowing that He is Enough for me. I have been working to look deep within myself to give God full reign and help me get rid of anything which could be preventing me from being free to allow Him to flow through me and bring forth the greatest potential He placed within me.

As I have been led by the Spirit of God, I have come to understand that I often felt invisible; Invisible to the world and always struggling to be seen. I simply wanted someone to see me, someone to understand that I do exist. Nothing more, nothing less, just to be seen for who I was becoming. I have been on an ever-evolving journey, coming to know who I am in Christ and knowing that He is Enough for me. I have been working to look deep within myself to give God full reign and help me get rid of anything which could be preventing me from being free to allow Him to flow through me and bring forth the greatest potential He placed within me.

As I journeyed with the Lord, I came to understand that I felt invisible, insignificant, and unloved. One day in another Encounter I saw Jesus being raised up on the cross and heard Him say these words to me: "They didn't see me either until I was raised up on the cross. I also was insignificant and unloved just like you feel." Tears streamed down my cheeks as I looked up into white light piercing my very being, penetrating deeply into my spirit, soul and body with His very presence. As I continued to watch Him, I saw a hand reach down and pull me out of the muck and mire I was stuck in. It was Jesus as Father God, reaching down to pull His baby girl up to Him. Next, I saw this wave of white light pour over me, washing away all my pain, bringing me life.

As I kept looking, I saw this beautiful white dress form on my little 12-year-old body and I was standing on the Father's feet, dancing. I was flowing with His rhythm and His grace, awed by His presence. He picked me up and held me above His head and I could look into His piercing eyes. He looked deep into my spirit, speaking these words into my heart: "I am proud of you." His eyes of love penetrated my very being, going deep into my soul and lifting me up above everything in the world.

I was then taken into another Encounter where the Father and I were on a horse and He placed me in front of Him. I was sorting through so many emotions in that moment as I experienced the trust of a Father, and the love of a Daddy for the first time. He was sitting behind me and He handed me the reins of the horse, saying: "go as fast as you can. Be free to ride the horse as hard as you want." I felt his hands wrap around my waist, holding onto me. His gentle touch pierced my being, touching deeper than hands can reach while lifting up my spirit, lifting up His little girl. The honor and the love I felt penetrating my entire being rose me to my feet. I saw myself standing up with a boldness, a confidence, and a courage to be Free. I heard my Daddy saying, "I have you Baby Girl and I won't let you fall!"

His hands were gentle and strong as He held me in place, perfectly balanced on this incredible creature. I saw the breath of God coming out of the horse as I stood firm in the identity of who I was becoming, feeling His touch holding me balanced. I let go of the reins in that moment, holding my hands out being completely free with the wind blowing through my hair and feeling the warmth of the sun on my face. This Encounter has become one of the most precious moments of my life.

I am free.

Yes, you are enough for me! You have touched my heart in a way where I know I am loved!

Opportunities to Renew Your Mind

What does it look like when you know God said "Go?"

What does it look like when your provisions do not yet match what is needed to fulfill what He has called you to complete?

What does it look like to rest in Jesus' arms as you walk out life and ministry?

What does it look like to not strive or stress?

Would you like to have some new tools from Heaven that could help you impact and shape culture?

God wants us each to find our own specific message that will reveal Jesus to others! The Lord wants you to be empowered to share your message so that other people will experience Jesus! "They overcame by the Blood of the Lamb, the Word of their testimony and not loving their lives unto death." (Revelation 12:11)

Do you believe that God wants to use you to touch someone else's life?

Take time to give language to your life experiences! You can help redefine what

Christianity looks like as you share with others the life message you have lived out while walking with God. It is time to shape our culture while we represent Jesus as truly Born Again Christians.

What if you could help the person you were speaking to have a life changing encounter with God by simply sharing what God put on your heart, just like Jesus did?

Learn how to sit with God and talk with Him about where He wants you to go each day to make a difference in just one person's life. Learn to wait on His presence to hear ways to share the life experiences you have stored away in your heart for such a time as this to change the lives of others dramatically. Learn how to effectively share with the one in front of you.

We are entering a time where the church needs to change in a way that will radically shift paradigms and change culture, bringing a whole new wave of Christianity into our world. Let's create a new wave of culture that will empower people to find their voice, to understand that the spiritual gifts are for everyone, and to help others realize Jesus lives inside of each of us. When Jesus lives inside of us, so do the Father and the Holy Spirit and we can allow the Living water inside of us to come alive and flow out of us, touching the lives of many broken people all throughout our communities.

Let's help people step beyond their fear of man and crush the fear of failure while learning how to minister to the one in front of them effectively. John and Peter represented Jesus well in Acts 3 and 4 by emulating Jesus. Let's also live lives that write additional chapters for the Book of Acts.

If you want to understand more of what this new season could look like and how to see change in your own community, learn how to see where God is moving and then speak life to His plans just like Jesus did when He only did what He saw the Father do and only said what the Father said. The time is now. Follow Jesus and let Him be enough for you.

References

References are taken from the Bible (NKJV, KJV, NIV, ESV, The Passion Translation)

Cover Design by Brandon Jordan
Edited by Edith Houghton

About the Author

Trina Olson is an Itinerant Minister founder of Radical Launch International Ministries, Inc. and co-founder of Unleashed Publishing, Inc. She is also co-founder of Flight Deck School of Supernatural Ministries and is in the process of starting Radical Launch Church. She received graduated from Global School of Supernatural Ministries under Dr. Randy Clark. She has also studied under Lou Engle at Ekballo School. She also attended Iris Leadership School in 2016-2017 school year. She has traveled to more than 33 states in the US and been on extended trips to Brazil, Costa Rica, Nicaragua, Dominican Republic, Guatemala, Belize, Kenya, Malawi, and Norway just in the last few years!

Trina's ministry, Radical Launch, reflects her heart to see others catapulted into their identity of Jesus Christ, Who will launch them into their destiny! She desires to see people encounter the one true living God through Jesus Christ, be filled with the Holy Spirit and walk out Isaiah 61 as Jesus calls us to heal the sick, cast out demons, bind up the broken, and raise the dead! She believes this is not just for a select few of people but for all! Her vision is to empower people to 'be in the game' as an important player making a difference in the lives of everyone they encounter! God radically transformed Trina's life in 2007 through a miraculous encounter with Himself! Her testimony is one of Divine intervention, inner and physical healing, and victory over spirits of depression and suicide that tried to take her life. God has given her a voice and a mandate to reach the youth of America with the message of the importance and power of a personal relationship with Jesus as she shares her story! He literally turned her life around that day and has set a fire inside of her that has taken her on an incredible journey with Him! She believes hearing someone else's testimony sets people free from their own bondage!

Trina has a dream from God and walking out that dream to launch others into their destiny. God is building a ministry out of relationship.

A bit of Revelation from Trina: You have a gold nugget inside of you to give to each person God puts in front of you. What you choose to do with that gold nugget is up to you. She learned that those gold nuggets are relationships. What if we have a part on earth to build the gold pavements of Heaven? We co-heir with Christ and if as we co-heir with Christ we love our God with all our heart, mind, spirit, and soul, and we love our neighbor as we love ourselves.

In addition to writing "Am I Enough for You", Trina has also written "Unleashed and Ready to Empower" and co-wrote "Radical Christianity 101".

Shores of Grace Ministries

❝The real ministry is to call others to the table.

Shores of Grace Ministries fights against human trafficking and prostitution and helps people in at-risk situations. Working in Brazil since 2010, we take the gospel to those around us through relationships in street evangelism, discipleship, and provide protection for children and adolescents in our rescue home. We want to see the restoration of individuals and families through God's revolutionary love. God is moving powerfully and we are seeing families restored and His table is being filled. God's desire all along has been to bless the earth through His family.

Nic & Rachael Billman
Founders and Directors of
Shores of Grace Ministries

Website: https://shoresofgrace.com

Hi, I'm Brandon Jordan. My beautiful wife, Rylee, and I live in Columbus Georgia where I've been all my life. I met Trina through a small home group we attended together as well as being connected at Grace Community Church in Fortson, Ga. I grew up with an obsession for drawing since early childhood. I won my first art competition in the 2nd grade, and it was then I knew I how much I enjoyed it. My dad was an artist at Fort Benning by profession, so I always paid close attention to his work along with getting him to do random sketches of me and the rest of our family when asked. He was always willing because he just loved drawing that much and THAT'S what rubbed off on me. I was always fascinated at just how much studying and hand technique he put into every drawing he did. He would just turn his head slowly side to side, eyes squinted, moving the paper back and forth as if he was looking through the lens of a camera keeping the image he was creating in focus and proportioned correctly. One rule of thumb he always made clear to me…"just slow down and enjoy the drawing". Another one he would say is "bring the portrait to life". From then on, one crumpled up sheet after another, from one sketch pad to the next, my personal style, which I always tried to copy my dads for years, developed into my own. I give all glory to God that he instilled this gift in me, but that he also gave me the grace and diligence to develop the talent through persistence. I'm so humbled and honored to have been personally asked to do this piece for Trina, and grateful that my talent is being used to bring Him to life on this book. I pray an abundance of blessings on all who invest in her story.

Empowering a Generation to have a voice

Unleashed publishing is opening doors to empower others to see their gifts and talents come alive. I have seen many of Brandon's drawings and his talent is amazing. I wasn't happy with the cover I had used and wanted something that would pop off the page and grab peoples attention. I feel the Auther usually has a great story but without the right cover or illustrations, it is just another book. The cover is the first thing that gets someones attention. The editor brings the book alive and with the convergence of the three you have a book that will leap off the shelf because it will satisfy the reader from cover to cover.

Thank you Brandon Jordon for your amazing gift and for creating an amazing work for me to use on my book "Am I Enough for You?".

Brandon is a freelancer and may be contacted through email: djbjordan1985@gmail.com

Unleashed Publishing, Inc.
Unleashing the potential authors, editors, and illustrators of a generation.

www.ingramcontent.com/pod-product-compliance
Lightning Source LLC
Chambersburg PA
CBHW041310110526
44590CB00028B/4312